Stock Trading Order Types

By

Bill Thompson

Copyright

© 2012 William F Thompson

ISBN-13: 978-1478289821

ISBN-10: 1478289821

Disclaimer

The information contained in this book is for informational and educational purposes only and is not to be considered investment advice.

Investing in stocks carries the potential for both gain and loss and investors pursuing any stock trading or investment strategy at times can and will lose money. Investors should seek out the advice of competent financial professionals to evaluate their particular needs and situation.

Investors should be aware that past performance is no indication of future results and there should be no assumption that any specific investment or investment strategy will be profitable or equal to past performance levels.

Forward

Although there are many resources and tools available in regards to what stocks to buy and sell, there are very few focused on the entering of the actual trade. Many investors spend years entering trades without fully knowing the use of available trading options like, 'Fill Or Kill', 'Immediate or Cancel', 'Do Not Reduce' as well as many others. A knowledge of all available options as well as how and when to use them can go a long way towards helping an investor achieve their goals and enhance their returns. The material in this book is geared towards both new and experienced investors alike and will allow them to take full advantage of all that is available to them.

About the Author

Bill Thompson has over 35 years experience as a stockbroker and trader and gained his knowledge of trading and order types working on the floor of the New York Stock Exchange as well as at some of the world's largest securities firms.

Table of Contents

Chapter 1 – Principles of Stocks

The First Stocks

Stocks are an ownership interest in a company. The origin of the name is obscure but is believed to derive from the Old English word, 'Stoc' (related to the Dutch 'Stok') meaning a block of wood or tree trunk. Some early stock may have been issued on engraved blocks of wood leading to the name. Another possibility is that the cash provided by the initial offering of stock provided the foundation of a company as the trunk provides the foundation of a tree. A related word is 'stockade'.

Stocks have been around since at least the 13th century as evidenced by a stock certificate dated June 16th, 1288 granting the Bishop of Vasteras 1/8th ownership of the Swedish Stora Kopparberg Mining Company.

The earliest stock (then called a joint-stock) company in modern times is the English East India Company established with a charter from Queen Elizabeth I on December 31st, 1600. This was followed two years later by the Dutch East India Company whose shares were traded on the new Amsterdam Stock Exchange. The establishment of stock exchanges enhanced the ability of joint-stock companies to attract capital from investors as they now had a mechanism to dispose of their shares. (Based on source material from www.nyx.com)

Stock Symbols

A stock symbol (also known as a ticker symbol from the old ticker tape machines) is an abbreviation used to identify the shares of a publicly traded company. Most symbols are one to four letters with a fifth letter sometimes added to identify a specific circumstance.

Most symbols reflect the name of the company such as 'DIS' for the Walt Disney Company and 'MCD' for McDonalds but sometimes the firm requests a symbol to identify some aspect of the company such as the Molson Coors Brewing Company using 'TAP' and Steinway Musical Instruments using 'LVB' for Ludwig van Beethoven.

Stock Exchanges and the Over-The–Counter Market

A stock exchange is a physical location where traders gather and trade stocks for their clients with the prices set by supply and demand. The largest and best-known exchange is the New York Stock Exchange.

The Over-The-Counter (or OTC) market is a market where traders (called Market Makers) trade through a computer network and are not face-to-face as with a stock exchange. The largest and best-known OTC market is NASDAQ, which stands for 'National Association of Securities Dealers Automated Quotations'. Today, it is usually written as 'Nasdaq' and is considered a proper name.

Types of Stock

There are three basic types of stock: Common, Preferred, and Treasury.

Common Stock

The vast majority of stock is common stock and is called that due to the common company ownership interest of the shareholders. Most common stock is Class A, which usually means that it has full voting rights in the company in regards to voting on a Board of Directors, approving large matters such as a merger with another company etc. There may also be other classes such as Class B, Class C etc. that have more limited or no voting rights. If a stock is simply called 'stock' then it is usually referring to Class A Common Stock.

Preferred Stock

A preferred stock is a stock that is given preference in regards to items such as a profit distribution (called a dividend) if one is declared by the Board of Directors. There are actually many types of preferred stock and their attributes can vary depending on the company. In the early part of the 20th century preferred stocks were more prevalent but today they are a very small part of the overall market and most stock investors deal exclusively with common shares.

Treasury Stock

This is stock (usually common) that a company has bought back off of the open market and keeps in its vaults (treasury). The stock can be resold on the open market at current prices at any time. Treasury stock may also refer to unissued shares.

Bull and Bear Markets

When stock markets are on an extended upwards trend they are called Bull Markets. An extended downwards trend is called a Bear Market.

There are different stories as to where the terms come from but most likely they are simply due to the fact that a bull pushes upwards with its horns when it attacks while a bear claws downwards.

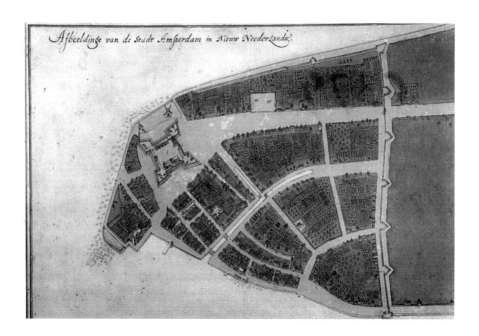

One of the earliest maps of Dutch New Amsterdam that became
English New York in 1664. Towards the right of the map is the wall
that gave Wall Street its name. It was constructed to provide
protection against the Native Americans and the English Military.
The text at the top reads, 'Image of the City Amsterdam in New
Netherland'. Source: Biblioteca Mediciea-Laurenziana of Florence,
Italy.

Chapter 2 – Stock Prices and Quotes

Basic Quotes

Stocks quote in dollars and cents (ex. 20.35 is $20.35). Stocks are usually quoted at the price of the last trade and this price is compared to the previous trading day's closing price.

Example: The Home Depot, Inc (Symbol HD) closed on Friday at $47.10. On Monday, the stock is trading at $48.50. If someone is quoting Home Depot they would normally say that it is trading at $48.50, up $1.40.

Besides the last trade, there are actually two other prices for a stock, the selling price and the buying price.

The Bid is the lower price and the Ask is the higher price. Basically, the Bid is the current price at which an investor can sell their stock and the Ask is the price at which they can buy the stock.

Example: Kellogg Co. (Symbol K) has the following quote:
Bid 50.25
Ask 50.27
Last Trade 50.26 up .21
Volume 156,500
Previous Close 50.05
Size 5 x 6

In general terms, the way to read this is that a middleman (a trader for an exchange listed stock and a market maker for a Nasdaq stock) is willing to pay $50.25 for the stock if an investor would like to sell it. They are asking $50.27 for the stock if an investor would like to buy it. The difference of $.02 is their profit margin and is called the spread.

Please note that when the market is open (9:30 a.m. to 4:00 p.m. EST) the Bid and Ask will change constantly although the change is usually not too drastic in the short run during a normal trading day. In a fast moving market however, this can change rapidly and what is shown on a quote may no longer be valid.

The last trade was at $50.26, which is up 21 cents from the previous trading day's last trade of $50.05.

The volume represents the number of shares that have traded so far during the current trading day.

Size refers to how many shares (in hundreds) are available at the Bid and Ask. A Size of 5 x 6 means that there are 500 shares available at the Bid and 600 shares at the Ask. As with the Bid and Ask, this number changes constantly.

Until April 2001 stocks traded and were quoted in 1/8's of a dollar with 1/8 representing 12 ½ cents. When the New York Stock Exchange was founded in 1792, the currency in use was Spanish Pieces of Eight. Today, stocks are quoted in dollars and cents.

Spanish Pieces of Eight. The original currency of the New York Stock Exchange. Source: Courtesy of the Author.

Another word used for dollars is points. If a stock is trading at $32.50 up $1, it is sometimes said to be 'trading up a point'.

Expanded Quotes

Here is a quote on Intel Corporation (symbol INTC) as it might appear on a webpage.

Last Trade: 26.07 -0.12 (-0.46%)
Prev Close: 26.19
Open: 26.24
Bid: 26.07
Ask: 26.09
Size: 180 x 100
Beta: 1.07
Day's Range: 26.05 – 26.57
52wk Range: 19.16 – 29.27
Volume: 43,444,810
Avg Vol (3m): 36,692,200
Market Cap: 131.16B

EPS (ttm): 2.36
P/E (ttm): 11.05
Div & Yield: 0.84 (3.22%)

Here's a breakdown of the different components.

Last Trade: 26.07 -0.12 (-0.46%)

This is the last reported trade as well as how much the stock is up or down compared to the last trade on the previous trading day. It is reported on a dollar and cents basis as well as a percent change.

Prev Close: 26.19

This was the last trade on the previous trading day during regular market hours. This does not report trades in the After-Hours Market that will be discussed in a subsequent chapter.

Open: 26.24

This was the first trade of the current trading day. Notice that this is different from the previous close. Stocks do not especially open at the same price that they close at. If there is no major news on the company or overall market then stocks will tend to open near where they close but if there is major news on either the company or the overall market then stocks can open considerably higher or lower. Subsequent chapters will discuss the order types to enter to help mitigate this risk.

Bid: 26.07
Ask: 26.09

As discussed previously, this shows what a market maker (INTC is a Nasdaq stock) is willing to pay for INTC stock (the Bid of $26.07) as well as what they are willing to sell it for (the Ask of $26.09) The difference of $.02 is their profit margin and is called the spread.

Size: 180 x 100

This shows how many shares (in hundreds) are available at the Bid and Ask. A size of 180 x 100 means that there are 18,000 shares available at the Bid (just add two zeros) and 10,000 shares at the Ask. As with the Bid and Ask, this number changes constantly.

Beta: 1.07

Beta is a measure of a stock's historical volatility compared to the overall market, in many cases as measured by the Standard and Poor's 500 Index. A stock with a Beta of 1.00 has tended to go up and down the same amount as the overall market. As an example, if the S&P 500 went up 10% then the stock went up 10% and if the S&P 500 went down 5% then the stock went down 5%. A stock with a Beta of 2.0 went up and down twice as much as the overall market and a stock with a Beta of 0.50 only half as much. The Beta of 1.07 shown here indicates that in the past Intel has been just slightly more volatile than the overall market. An important point to note is that Beta is based on past performance and may not be an indication of the future.

Day's Range: 26.05 – 26.57

This shows how high and low the stock has traded during the current trading day.

52wk Range: 19.16 – 29.27

This shows the range of the stock's trading over the last year, going back one year from today or one year from yesterday, depending on the quote service.

Volume: 43,444,810

This shows how many shares have traded today.

Avg Vol (3m): 36,692,200

This shows the average daily trading volume for the last three months. If an investor sells 100 shares of stock to another investor or market maker, it counts as 100 shares, not 200. The buy and sell are counted as the same 100 shares. Some investors compare the current day's trading volume to the average as a potential buy or sell signal.

Market Cap: 131.16B

This stands for 'Market Capitalization' and is a reflection of the company's value on the stock market. It is calculated by multiplying the company's current stock price by the number of shares of stock that make up the company (this number can be found in the company's 'Key Statistics' and is not normally listed as part of the quote).

The 131.16B Market Cap means that Intel is valued on the stock market at $131.16 Billion Dollars ($131,160,000,000).

EPS (ttm): 2.36

EPS stands for 'Earnings Per Share' and ttm means 'trailing twelve months'. This number reports that Intel earned a profit of $2.36 per share over the last year and is calculated by dividing the total profit by the number of outstanding shares.

P/E (ttm): 11.05

This is the Price/Earnings Ratio and is one of the most common comparison of two numbers looked at by investors. It is calculated by dividing the current share price by the last twelve month's Earnings Per Share. (Example: $26.07/$2.36 = 11.05).

The way to read this is that an investor is paying $11.05 for each dollar of profit. What is considered a good P/E ratio can vary depending on the industry and also on the general level of interest rates. In high interest rate environments, investors are willing to pay less for each dollar of profits, resulting in a lower acceptable P/E, as there are alternative places to earn a good return such as bonds. In low interest rate environments, investors are willing to pay more for each dollar of profits and find higher P/E's acceptable.

Companies with stable earnings such as utilities tend to trade at higher P/E ratios than companies with more volatile earnings such as auto stocks.

An important point to note with P/E ratios is that they are based on past earnings that may or may not occur in the future.

Div & Yield: 0.84 (3.22%)

Div is short for 'Dividend' and is that portion of the company's profits that have been paid out to shareholders over the past year. The yield is the dividend divided by the current share price (Example: $0.84/$26.07 = 3.22%)

Conclusion

Successful trading involves many steps but one of the most important foundations is the proper reading and understanding of quotes.

Chapter 3 – Stock Splits

Stock Splits

Standard Stock Splits

Stock splits are simply when an investor receives additional shares for each share they currently own. The most common stock split is a 2 for 1 split where an investor ends up with two shares for each one they currently own with each share trading at ½ the previous price. Technically what happens is that they receive one additional share for each share currently owned (this is a 100% stock dividend). Most investors just think of it as if they simply doubled their shares. The key is that they end up with twice as many shares at ½ the price. The total value of the investment does not change.

The primary reason that most companies split their stock is to make it appear more affordable. Investors generally prefer to buy stocks between $20 and $80 a share and sometimes shy away from stocks over $100 a share so splits can increase marketability. Companies also sometimes split their stocks to increase the number of shares outstanding. This can help with liquidity and also be effective in fending off a hostile take over attempt, which is when one company makes an unsolicited attempt to acquire more than 50% of another firm's stock.

Calculating Post Split Share Quantity and Price

To determine how many shares an investor will have after a split and at what price, the key is to remember that the total value of the investment does not change. The below example illustrates the process.

Example: An investor owns 100 shares of stock valued at $120 a share. The total value of the investment is 100 X $120 = $12,000.

The company announces a 3 for 2 split. This means that after the split the investor will have 3 shares for every 2 currently owned.

To calculate the new number of the shares, multiply the current share quantity by the split amount written as a fraction. (ex. a 3 for 2 split would be 3/2, a 5 for 4 split would be 5/4)

Since this is a 3 for 2 split, we multiply the existing 100 shares by 3 divided by 2.

100 shares x 3/2 = 300/2 = 150 shares

To calculate the new share price, multiply the current price by the inverse (turn it upside down) of the fraction we just used.

Since our share price is $120 a share and the inverse of the fraction used for the share quantity is 2/3 our formula is:

$120 x 2/3 = 240/3 = $80

To summarize:

Before the split

100 shares @ $120 a share = $12,000

After the 3 for 2 split

150 shares @ $80 a share = $12,000

It's always a good idea to double check the numbers by making sure the total value remains the same.

Reverse Stock Splits

Occasionally a company will do a reverse stock split. This is usually done to increase the value of a low-priced stock to make it appear less risky.

Example:

A company whose stock price is $2 a share declares a 1 for 10 reverse split. For every 10 shares that an investor has at $2, they will end up with 1 share at $20.

A problem with reverse splits is that it is somewhat cosmetic and the company still hasn't dealt with the issues that caused the stock to decline to $2 in the first place.

Wall Street in 1847 with Trinity Church (next picture) in the background. Source: United States Library of Congress.

Trinity Church at the end of Wall Street. This active Episcopal church dates back to 1846 with its two predecessors at the same location since 1697. Photograph by the author.

Chapter 4 – Order Fulfillment

Order Fulfillment

When placing an order through a brokerage firm, the brokerage firm has four basic options as to how to fill the order.

The order can be sent to an exchange.

The order can be directed to a market maker.

The order can be sent to an ECN.

The order can be filled internally.

Order routing is automated at brokerage firms and is usually a fast process. Brokerage firms are obligated to fill client orders at the best available price.

Many brokerage firms give investors the option to direct how they would like their order filled although some may charge an extra fee to do so.

Sending the order to an exchange

For a stock that is listed on an exchange such as the New York Stock Exchange, the firm may route the order directly to that exchange. The firm also has the option to send the order to another exchange, such as a regional exchange, if a better price is quoted.

Directing the order to a market maker

For an exchange-listed stock, the brokerage firm also has the option to direct the order to another firm called, a 'third market maker'. This is a firm that stands ready to buy and sell an exchange-listed stock at the publicly quoted prices.

An important point to note is that many regional exchanges and third market maker's pay brokerage firms to route orders to them. This is called, 'payment for order flow' and is generally in the range of about a penny a share.

Brokerage firms must state on trade confirmations as to whether they received payment for order flow. Many brokerage firms state that the payments they receive for order flow allow them to offer more services to investors at lower prices. Regardless of where the order fills, brokerage firms are still obligated to fill orders at the best available price.

The process is similar for Nasdaq stocks. Since these stocks are not listed on exchanges, all orders are sent to market makers. Nasdaq market makers may also pay for order flow.

Sending the order to an electronic communications network.

Electronic communications networks (ECN's) are computer networks that allow brokerage firms, institutions such as pension plans, as well as at times individual investors to trade directly with each other without a middleman such as a market maker. ECN's can automatically match buy and sell orders and eliminate or split the spread between the Bid and Ask price.

Filling an order internally

This is known as 'internalization' and is when a brokerage firm fills a client's order out of its own inventory. Some firms may also do cross matching of their clients buy and sell orders to split the spread between the Bid and Ask and obtain better prices for both.

Example: Proctor & Gamble (PG) has the following quote:

Last Trade: 62.39

Bid: 62.39

Ask: 62.41

An investor entering an order to sell 100 shares at the prevailing price (called a Market Order) would receive $62.39 per share while an investor at the same firm buying 100 shares would pay $62.41. The spread of $.02 would normally go to a floor trader or market maker.

The firm may match the orders in the middle at $62.40 and give both investors a better price. The firm would still make money based on the commission charged for the trades.

The World's Major Stock Exchanges in 1886. Clockwise from the top left: New York (the predecessor to the current building that opened in 1903), Paris, Chicago, Brussels, Berlin, Frankfurt, Hamburg, with London in the middle. Today, there are stock exchanges around the world with the largest being the New York, London, and Tokyo Stock Exchanges. Source: United States Library of Congress.

Chapter 5 – The After-Hours Market

The After-Hours Market

Regular trading hours are generally considered to be Monday through Friday from 9:30 a.m. to 4:00 p.m. Eastern Time. These are the operating hours for both the New York Stock Exchange and Nasdaq.

Many brokerage firms offer after-hours trading through ECN's that match buy and sell orders. The after-hour services can vary from brokerage firm to brokerage firm so it is important for investors interested in after-hours trading to research what each firm offers in regards to the hours that trading is available as well as which ECN's the firm uses.

A common misconception by investors is that they can obtain that day's regular market close price in the after-hours market even when there is significant news on a company. In reality, the after-hours market share prices will generally adjust upwards for positive news and downwards for negative news and investors will even at times pay more for a buy and obtain less for a sell than if they had waited until the next day's open. This can be due to the lower trading activity of the after-hours market.

Risks of After-Hours Trading

There are several risks to after-hours trading.

Inability to trade on all ECN's – An investor's brokerage firm may not trade on all ECN's in the after-hours market so an investor may see a better price on another ECN but not be able to trade on it. A buy and sell order may be entered at identical prices on different ECN's and not be able to execute.

Wider spreads between the Bid and Ask – The lower trading activity in the after-hours market may result in higher spreads between the Bid and Ask resulting in lower available prices for sellers and higher prices for buyers.

Greater price volatility – The more limited trading activity tends to cause stock prices to fluctuate more in the after-hours market, particularly as investors attempt to disseminate after-hours news.

Lack of Liquidity – The limited trading in the after-hours market may make it difficult to fill large orders and some stocks may not trade at all.

Competition with institutions – A large part of the after-hours market is trading between institutions such as mutual funds and pension plans and they may have the staffing and resources available to more quickly analyze market data and act on it.

Summary of After-Hours Trading

Although after-hours trading can in some circumstances be an important resource to investors, the recognition of the additional risks should be considered when making trading decisions.

The New York Stock Exchange in an 1882 painting by Hughson Hawley. The move to the larger, current building located a few doors down on Broad Street occurred in 1903.
Source: United States Library of Congress.

Chapter 6 – Market and Limit Orders

Market and Limit Orders

The two most basic types of orders are Market and Limit Orders.

Market Order

Market orders are an order to buy or sell a stock at the current market price. An order to buy would purchase the stock at the current Ask price and an order to sell would be at the current Bid price.

A market order is guaranteed to go through since the order says to buy or sell at whatever the market price is. The problem is that the price may change between when the order is entered and when it is filled (executed). If the markets are open and the stock appears to be stable then usually the order will fill at close to the prevailing price but there is never a guarantee.

Market orders can be placed any time of the day or night and also on weekends and holidays but if the markets are not open then the order will fill at or near the opening price the next time the market opens.

It is important to reiterate that stocks do not especially open at the same price that they close at. If there is no news on the stock and no significant news to move the overall market then a stock will tend to open near where it closed but it is not a guarantee.

To sum up, Market Orders guarantee that you will buy or sell the stock but the price is not guaranteed.

Limit Order

A Limit Order is an order in which an investor sets the price that they would like to buy or sell the stock at. With a buy order, the investor is hoping that the stock will come down to their price in which case the order will automatically fill and with a sell order they are hoping that the stock will come up to their price.

Example

An investor is looking to buy 100 shares of Starbucks (SBUX).

Starbucks is currently trading at $54.89 and the investor thinks the stock is going to drop before going back up so the investor enters an order to buy 100 shares of Starbucks at a limit of $54.00. What this means is that the investor is placing an order to buy 100 shares of Starbucks if the price drops to $54.00 (Since this is a buy order the Ask actually has to drop to $54.00). The order will fill automatically so the investor does not have to constantly watch the stock.

An advantage of a limit order is that if Starbucks goes down to $54.00 the investor saves $.89 per share, ($89 for the total order of 100 shares) as opposed to buying at market.

A disadvantage of a limit order is that Starbucks may never drop to $54.00 and just goes up in which case the investor never buys the stock.

A Market Order guarantees the purchase or sale but doesn't guarantee the price whereas a Limit Order guarantees the price but doesn't guarantee the purchase or sale.

A sell limit order works the same way except that the investor is trying to sell their stock at a higher price than the current market. If the investor is correct and the stock goes up then they will receive more proceeds but if the stock does not go up then the trade will not execute and they may have to eventually sell at a lower price.

Day Order vs. Good Until Canceled Order (GTC)

An order can be placed for either one trading day (if the markets are closed the order is interpreted to be for the next trading day) or Good-Til-Canceled (many times stated as Good Until Canceled), in which case it's in place for a certain time limit (typically 60 calendar days but this can vary by brokerage firm). Market orders are automatically assumed to be day orders.

Until a limit order executes an investor is free to cancel or change the order.

Wall Street in 1797. The building on the left is the Tontine Coffee House that was the first permanent home of the New York Stock Exchange. From a 1797 Oil on Linen painting by Francis Guy. Source: New York Public Library.

Chapter 7 – Or Better Orders

Or Better Orders

Another type of order is an Or Better Order. This is effectively a market order with a limit aspect included. These orders are effective if placing an order when the market is closed or with a volatile (called fast moving) stock.

Unlike a Buy Limit Order where an investor places a limit below the current market price, with an Or Better Order the investor is placing a limit price above the current market price stating that this is the absolute maximum they are willing to pay for the stock. The brokerage firm is still obligated to buy the stock at the lowest available price but if the stock is above the investors stated limit then the order will not execute unless the stock returns to the limit price.

Example

An investor wants to buy 1,000 shares of Microsoft (MSFT). Microsoft finished the day at $29.08 and released good earnings news after the market closed. The investor would like to buy Microsoft the next morning when the market opens but they will be at work and will not have an opportunity to monitor the stock as it opens. With the good earnings news the investor knows that there is a strong possibility that Microsoft will open higher than the $29.08 closing price.

The investor would like to buy the stock as inexpensively as possible but decides that they are willing to pay up to $32.50 a share if necessary.

The investor places an order to buy 1,000 shares of MSFT at a price of $32.50 Or Better. The Or Better means Or Better for the investor.

If the stock opens at any price at or below $32.50 then that is the price the investor will pay (They will actually pay the Ask Price). If the stock opens higher (Ex. $32.90) then the order remains as a normal limit order with no fill unless the stock drops back to $32.50. The investor is always free to cancel an unfilled order.

As an example, if Microsoft opens at $30.75, then that is the price the investor will pay. Just because they entered a limit of $32.50 doesn't mean that is what they pay. That is just the maximum price that they indicated they are willing to pay, if necessary. Their brokerage firm is still obligated to purchase the stock for them at the lowest possible price.

As another example, let's assume that an investor owns 700 shares of eBay (EBAY). The stock closed at $37.50 and the market is now closed. The investor would like to place an order to sell their stock the next day but doesn't want to take the risk of a market order. The investor has a good profit and decides that they will accept a minimum of $35.75 although they would obviously like to sell the stock for as high a price as possible.

The investor places an order to sell the 700 shares as an Or Better order with a minimum price of $35.75.

The stock opens at $37.87 and this is the price their shares sell for since it's above their minimum acceptable price.

Again, the 'Or Better' means better for the investor. The investor's brokerage firm is still obligated to sell the stock at the highest possible price as long as it is above the minimum price set by the investor.

If the investor were looking to sell eBay at a higher price than the current market (Ex. $40) they would enter a simple limit order.

As with Limit Orders, Or Better Orders can be entered as either Day Orders or GTC.

Chapter 8 – Fill or Kill and Immediate or Cancel Orders

Fill or Kill and Immediate or Cancel

Fill or Kill and Immediate or Cancel orders are not used too often but are entered on occasion. They are used in a situation where an investor wishes to place a near market limit order to save a few pennies per share but needs a quick answer.

Fill or Kill

A Fill or Kill order is a form of a limit order but instead of a Day Order or GTC order it is entered for just a few minutes. It is used to make an offer to a floor trader or market maker with the objective of getting an immediate yes or no answer. The following example will illustrate.

An investor sees the following quote on Wal-Mart (WMT).

68.70 Bid   68.74 Ask

The Investor is looking to purchase 2,000 shares but rather than enter a market order they try to see if they can save a few pennies off the 68.74 Asking price. They decide to enter an order to buy 2,000 shares at 68.72 but rather than a day order they enter Fill or Kill (FOK). Our investor knows that Wal-Mart is about to release earnings after the close and doesn't want to take a chance with a Day Limit Order not filling as they want to own the stock before the close. They need an immediate answer from a floor trader so they can make a decision on how to proceed. A Fill or Kill order says to fill the entire order or none of it. It does not allow for partial fills.

One of two things will happen with a Fill or Kill order. The trader will fill it in its entirety (Fill) or they will reject the entire order (Kill) and send it back as Nothing Done (ND). Our investor will now have their answer and they can decide to either re-enter the order as a market order or a limit with a higher price or do nothing at all.

Immediate or Cancel

An Immediate or Cancel (IOC) order is the same as Fill or Kill except that it allows for partial fills. In other words, the investor is saying to the trader, "Give me as many shares as you can immediately and cancel the rest."

Caution Areas With Fill or Kill and Immediate or Cancel orders

Years ago an investor could usually get an answer on a FOK or IOC order within 2 to 5 minutes. Nowadays, with the higher trading volumes it can sometimes take up to 20 to 30 minutes to get an answer at which time the stock has usually moved so FOK and IOC orders are not used as much today although they can still be effective with thinly traded stocks with a big spread between the Bid and Ask. An investor's brokerage firm may be able to give them an idea as to how fast they usually resolve FOK and IOC orders.

The New York Stock Exchange. The NYSE is by far the world's largest stock exchange in terms of dollar trading value. The front wall behind the columns and flag is actually made of glass. Photograph by the author.

Chapter 9 – Stop Orders

Stop Orders

Stop orders are the one order investor's hope will not fill. They are entered in an attempt to potentially stop losses and are sometimes called Stop Loss orders although this is incorrect, as they do not always stop a loss.

They are usually entered when an investor owns a stock that they want to continue to hold as long as it goes up but want some protection in case it goes down. The investor enters a sell order that only executes if the stock declines to a stated price (called the stop price). One trade at or below the stop price turns the order into a market order. The example should clarify.

Example

An investor owns 100 shares of Walt Disney Inc. (DIS) stock. The stock is currently at $50.59 and the investor wishes to continue to hold the stock as long as it goes up. The investor is going on vacation and is concerned that the stock may decline so they issue a stop order at $45. What this means is that if there is one trade on DIS at or below $45 then the order will become active to sell 100 shares at market.

In a normal trading day the shares should sell close to $45. The order becomes active with the first trade at or below $45 so as soon as the first trade at $45 occurs it is a market order and the stock should sell quickly at the market price that may be right at $45 or slightly below or above depending on the market movement once the order becomes active.

The problem occurs if the stock gaps down overnight. Let's assume that the stock closed one day at $45.75. After the close of trading there is negative earnings news and the first trade the next day is at $41. The stop order to sell said that it becomes a market order with the first trade at or below $45 and since $41 is the first trade that fulfills this condition then the order becomes a market order to sell which would occur at or near $41.

This may not have been the investor's intent although if the stock continues to decline they may be happy with the $41 price.

Stop Limit Order

As another option the investor could enter a stop limit order. This is similar to a stop order except in addition to the stop trigger price, the investor also sets a bottom price limit, below which they will not accept.

Using the previous example, the investor could enter an order with a stop of $45 and a limit of $43.25. The investor is saying that with any trade at or below $45, sell at market but not for less than $43.25. In a normal trading day, if the stock declined to $45 then the order would execute at market, which would probably be at or near $45 so both conditions are met. If however, the stock gapped down to $41 then the order has been made active since the $45 trigger has been reached (think of a stop price as turning on a light switch for an order) but the order will not fill until the second condition of $43.25 has been reached. In other words, it is a simple limit order. If the stock goes back up to $43.25 then the order will fill but if the stock continues to decline then the order will never fill.

Chapter 10 – Special Conditions

Special Conditions

There are three Special Conditions that are sometimes used when entering stock orders.

They are:

Minimum Quantity

All or None

Do Not Reduce

Minimum Quantity

Minimum Quantity is used when entering Limit Orders where an investor wants to set a minimum quantity in the event their order is filled in different lots (amounts).

As an example, let's say that our investor wishes to purchase 1,000 shares of Mattel (MAT) at 35.10. Rather than take a chance on getting filled 100 shares one day and then 100 shares the next and so on where the investor might pay multiple commissions, the investor enters their order as Buy 1,000 shares MAT Limit 35.10 Minimum Quantity 300. This tells their brokerage firm to not fill the order for less than 300 shares at a time. This restriction applies to all except the last fill, which can be in any quantity to complete the order.

An example of how this order might fill would be with a first lot of 500 shares, a second lot of 300 shares and a final lot of 200 shares to complete the transaction.

All or None

All or None simply states to either fill the entire order at once (All) or none at all (None). Depending on the size of the order, sometimes an All or None (AON) will not fill even if the stock is at the limit price since the trader cannot fill the entire quantity. As a general rule, it's usually best to put as few restrictions as possible on orders to give the brokerage firm the maximum flexibility to fill.

Minimum Quantity or All or None are not accepted on market orders since market orders by their nature state to fill the entire order regardless of price.

Do Not Reduce

When a company pays a dividend, the share price is immediately reduced by the amount of the dividend. As an example, if a stock closed last night at $58 a share and that was the last day to purchase to receive an upcoming $1 dividend then the next morning (all other things being equal) the stock will open at $57. This could create a problem for an investor who might have a limit order placed to buy at $57.25. Their order would fill since the stock is trading below their limit price (they would actually fill at $57, not $57.25 since orders have to be filled at the most advantageous price to the investor).

An order filling just because of a price move related to a dividend may not be the investor's intent so to avoid this brokerage firms automatically adjust all buy orders by the amount of the dividend. The investors Buy Limit at $57.25 would be adjusted down to a Buy Limit at $56.25. If the investor does not want this to happen then they would enter their limit order with the special condition Do Not Reduce (DNR). Most investors do not use this qualifier but it is available if needed.

Round Lot vs. Odd Lot

A Round Lot is a name for increments of 100 shares. Anything from 1 to 99 shares is called an Odd Lot. An order to sell 457 shares of stock would be considered four Round Lots of 100 shares and one Odd Lot of 57 shares. Years ago, Odd Lot purchase orders filled at 1/8th of dollar higher than round lots (the investor paid more) and Odd Lot sell orders filled at 1/8th of a dollar less. This no longer applies so there is no real distinction between Round Lots and Odd Lots.

Settlement

Settlement refers to how long it takes an investor to receive their money after selling a stock and how long before they have to pay for a purchase. Settlement on stock is currently three business days. The way this works is to start with the next business day after the trade and count to three (T+3), skipping holidays and weekends.

Example: If an investor buys a stock on Monday then they have to pay for it by the close of business on Thursday (start with the next business day (Tuesday) after the trade and count to three). The third day (Thursday) is settlement day.

Example: If an investor sells a stock on Thursday, then their money is available to them on Tuesday, which is settlement day. They can usually receive proceeds at the start of business on settlement day. The way settlement day is arrived at in this case is to start with the next business day after the trade (Friday) and count to three skipping the weekends.

Please note that settlement on Mutual Funds is currently one day. Most brokerage firms require that the funds be in the account before allowing a mutual fund purchase order since settlement is the next day. Subsequently, if an investor sells a mutual fund then the proceeds are available to them the next business day, usually at the start of business.

NEW YORK STOCK EXCHANGE, NEW YORK CITY.

An accurate portrayal of the New York Stock Exchange. The front of the building actually faces Broad Street with Wall Street to the right of the tower. Source: United States Library of Congress.

Chapter 11 – Short Selling

Short Selling

Most of the time investors purchase stock with the expectation that the stock price is going to go up. Basically this is the strategy of buy low and sell high. Sometimes however, an investor will use a strategy called short selling to try and make money on a stock when it goes down.

Short Selling Mechanics

Let's assume that an investor has reason to think that Macy's (M) stock is about to go down. Macy's is currently trading at $48 a share. The investor has a cousin who owns 100 shares of Macy's that they keep as a long-term investment and they have the stock certificate in a safe deposit box at a bank. The investor asks their cousin if they can borrow their certificate for a few weeks. The cousin agrees and signs the certificate over to the investor. The investor then immediately sells the 100 shares of stock and receives proceeds of $4,800 (They would actually pay a commission but for the purposes of the example we are going to disregard commissions).

The investor is correct and the stock goes down to $30 a share. The investor does not believe Macy's is going to go any lower so they purchase back the 100 shares for $3,000 and ask that the certificate be made out to their cousin. They then return the certificate. The investor made $1,800 on the transaction.

To sum up:

1) Investor borrows 100 shares of Macy's and sells the stock for $48 a share. Receives proceeds of $4,800.

2) Stock goes down to $30 and investor repurchases the 100 shares for $3,000. Investor returns stock and makes a profit of $1,800.

This is the strategy of Buy Low and Sell High except that the sell occurred before the buy.

Basically, the investor made money using borrowed stock. When an investor owns an investment they are considered to have a long position. Most investors simply buy stock and then own it so they are considered long in the stock. When an investor sells borrowed stock they are considered to be 'short' the stock since they eventually have to give it back. This is a short position.

Disadvantages of Short Selling

Short Selling works fine if a stock goes down. The problem is if it goes up. When an investor buys a stock and takes a long position there is a limit to how much money they can lose since a stock cannot go below $0. Since there is no theoretical limit as to how high a stock can go an investor who short sells a stock is taking on potentially unlimited losses.

The following example will illustrate.

Let's assume that an investor borrows 1,000 shares of Johnson & Johnson (JNJ) and sells the stock at $67 a share. Their proceeds are $67,000. Instead of going down however, the stock starts to go up and when the stock is at $120 our investor receives a request to return the stock. The investor has to repurchase the stock for $120,000 and suffers a loss of $53,000.

Technical Aspects of Short Selling

Some investors short sell and make money doing so but since historically the markets go up more than they go down an investor has to be careful. For our example, we assumed the investor borrowed stock from a relative but in reality they usually borrow it from their brokerage firm. Generally, there is no interest charged and no specific time limit as to how long the stock can be borrowed but most brokerage firms reserve the right to demand that the stock be returned at any time if necessary (this is a 'call in' or 'forced buy back') although this rarely happens. What usually happens is the brokerage firm will require larger deposits of cash to be kept in the account in the event the stock goes up and potential losses grow.

It is also not advisable to short sell low priced stocks since the profit potential is limited in relation to the potentially unlimited losses. As an example, if an investor shorts 100 shares of a $6 stock their maximum potential profit is $600 since the stock can't go below $0 and yet they are taking on potentially unlimited losses if it goes up.

An investor must also have a margin account to short sell stocks. Margin trading is discussed in the next chapter. Only marginable stocks are eligible for short selling. Most stocks below $5 a share are not marginable so they usually are not eligible.

Stop Orders and Short Selling

Investors can also use stop orders when they have a short position. Basically they are saying to buy back the stock if the price rises to a certain stated price. Again there is always the danger that the stock can gap up overnight on good news. The investor can also place a second limit above their trigger price, which is the maximum price they will pay to close out the short position. Again, the problem is the stock may gap above that price and continue to rise.

The figure at the center of the NYSE Pediment is called, 'Integrity' with the ten men, women, and children representing Invention, Science, Industry, Agriculture, and Mining. The Pediment is entitled, 'Integrity Protecting The Works of Man'. Photograph by the author.

Chapter 12 – Margin

Margin

Margin is using borrowed money to buy stock or taking a loan from a brokerage firm using the underlying stock as collateral. For most stocks margin is currently 50%. This rate is set by the Federal Reserve (not the Securities and Exchange Commission). The Federal Reserve has not changed margin since 1974.

Basically, margin of 50% means that you can purchase a stock by putting down 50% of the purchase price as a deposit and the brokerage firm will lend you the other 50%. You will pay interest on this borrowed money at whatever interest rate the brokerage firm has set. The interest rate can change depending on the general level of interest rates although most firms are under competitive pressure to keep rates relatively low.

Margin Example

Lets assume that an investor has $5,000 that they would like to invest in a stock trading at $50 a share. They would normally buy 100 shares and their total potential loss would be limited to the $5,000 investment.

As a second option, the investor decides to buy the stock on margin. Since margin is 50% they can purchase 200 shares ($10,000) with the investor putting down $5,000 and the brokerage firm lending them the other $5,000. With a pre-approved margin account this would happen automatically. Our investor now owns 200 shares as opposed to 100 shares with a straight cash purchase but their potential maximum loss is now $10,000 since if the stock goes to $0 they lose their $5,000 investment and still have to pay back the loan of $5,000 plus the interest.

Lets assume the stock goes up to $70 and the investor decides to sell. If the investor had made a cash purchase of 100 shares for $5,000 then they would have a profit of $2,000 ($7,000 - $5,000).

In the case of purchasing 200 shares on margin the investor would receive proceeds of $14,000 ($70 x 200 shares). After paying back the $5,000 loan the investor would receive total proceeds of $9,000, which is a profit of $4,000 on a $5,000 investment.

Here is a summary of the example.

$5,000 to invest in a $50 a share stock.

Cash Purchase

Buy 100 shares at $50 = $5,000

Loan = $0

Stock rises to $70

Sell 100 shares at $70 = $7,000

Loan = $0

Net proceeds = $7,000

Profit = $2,000

Margin Purchase

Buy 200 shares at $50 = $10,000

Loan = $5,000

Stock rises to $70

Sell 200 shares at $70 = $14,000

Repay loan of $5,000

Net proceeds = $9,000

Profit = $4,000

An investor using margin would also have to pay interest on the margin loan, which would decrease the profit somewhat.

Here is the example again assuming that the investor sells the stock after it declines to $30 a share.

$5,000 to invest in a $50 a share stock.

Cash Purchase

Buy 100 shares at $50 = $5,000

Loan = $0

Stock declines to $30

Sell 100 shares at $30 = $3,000

Loan = $0

Net proceeds = $3,000

Loss = $2,000

Margin Purchase

Buy 200 shares at $50 = $10,000

Loan = $5,000

Stock declines to $30

Sell 200 shares at $30 = $6,000

Repay loan of $5,000

Net proceeds = $1,000

Loss = $4,000

Basically, margin results in a greater profit if the stock goes up but results in a greater loss if the stock goes down. This is called 'leveraging'.

This is a general introduction to margin. For more comprehensive information, a good source is the website of the Securities and Exchange Commission.

Here is the link:

http://www.sec.gov/investor/pubs/margin.htm

The statue of George Washington looks out from the top of the steps of Federal Hall on Wall Street marking the exact location of the inauguration of General Washington as the first President of the United States on April 30th, 1789. Photograph by the author.

Chapter 13 – A Brief Commentary on Penny Stocks, Technical Analysis, and Options

A few words on some other subject areas related to stock trading.

Penny Stocks

Penny stocks (called cent stocks in some countries) are generally defined as stocks that trade for under $1.00 a share although the technical definition is for any stock whose shares trade for under $5. Although there can at times be good profit potential with penny stocks, they are generally considered speculative as many of them are thinly traded and may have large spreads between the Bid and Ask. They may also be subject to price manipulation.

Here is some more information on penny stocks from the Securities and Exchange Commission.

http://www.sec.gov/answers/penny.htm

Technical Analysis

Technical Analysis is the use of statistical variables such as price changes, trend analysis, volume changes etc. to try to identify and predict price movements in a stock. Charts are heavily used in technical analysis. Technical Analysis is a favorite tool of short-term traders in a stock (called Day Traders).

Options

Options are financial instruments whose value comes from the underlying movement of something else such as a stock or market index. Although options are primarily used by financial institutions for hedging and income enhancement strategies, they are also used by investors trying to make a relatively quick profit by correctly predicting the short and intermediate price movements of a stock or market index. Although investors speculating on the short-term movements of the markets can potentially make large profits, many end up losing their entire investment so caution is advised.

For more information on Options, in particular their value for individual investors in regards to hedging (protecting against loss) and income enhancement, a good source is the website of the Chicago Board Options Exchange www.cboe.com. Once there, simply click on the Education tab.

Chapter 14 – Ten Principles of Stock Trading and Stock Ownership

Ten Principles of Stock Trading and Stock Ownership

Here are some principles that I've observed in my many years as a stockbroker and stock trader that can help make for more successful stock trading and ownership.

Invest in what you know

When investing in a company for the long-term, an investor should have good knowledge of the company as well as its industry. This will help with the dissemination of news and the forecasting of future trends.

For short-term traders, it is important to have a good grasp as to the causes and trends of a company's past stock price movements in an attempt to forecast future movements. Remember that there is no guarantee that a stock price will move in the same way as it has in the past.

Know your risk tolerance

An investor should ask themselves what would happen if their investment suddenly lost half of its value. This may help in deciding what kind of risk can be taken on.

It doesn't have to be all at once

Rather than investing all at once, consideration could be given to investing part of the money now and the rest later. If the stock goes up, then some of the money is in at the lower price point. If the stock goes down, there would be an opportunity to average down. If the stock stays the same, there is an opportunity to decide if this is still the best place for the additional funds or are there now better opportunities available.

Buy and Hold is not Buy and Forget

Even if the investment is for the long-term, an investor will still want to keep an eye on the company and its industry as over time there may be fundamental changes that affect its long-term viability.

Have an exit strategy

Successful investors generally have a price point at which they will get out of a stock and move on to something else. It is difficult to recover from a stock whose price has declined from $100 to $3.

An example of a sell strategy is that if the stock price declines 20% from the purchase price or 25% from a new high, whichever occurs first, then it's time to move on. Each investor can set their own individual percentages. The key is to have some kind of plan.

Sell strategies should take into account tax implications as well as fees and commissions.

Investing in the company vs. trading the stock

If someone is a long-term investor, then they are investing in the company and as such, should become familiar with the company's fundamentals in regards to things like sales, profits, debt levels etc. Over time, the stock price will tend to reflect the company's performance rather than the day-to-day movements of the stock market which in the short-term can be based on emotion.

If an investor's outlook is short-term, then generally they are attempting to make money off of the short-term price movements of the stock and may not be as concerned with the fundamentals of the company. In this case most of their emphasis should focus on the technical short-term aspects of the stock price movement.

Do not become emotionally involved in the stock or company

It is easy to become emotionally attached to a company or stock, particularly if an investor has held it for a long time or are a fan of the company's products.

An investor should make every effort to step back and ask themselves if this is still the best place for their money or if there are now better opportunities available elsewhere.

Take into account tax considerations

An investor should always take into account the tax implications of any buy or sell order and should consult a qualified tax professional with any questions.

Keep an eye on fees and commissions

Many day traders tend to lose track of how much in commissions and fees they are actually paying. This is easy to do, particularly as money moves in and out of the overall account. An investor should keep careful track of all commissions and fees to make sure that their strategy is returning the desired results. They should also keep accurate records to help with tax form preparation.

Be ready for the four market scenarios

Most investor's think that the markets can only go up, down, or stay the same and may have strategies in place to deal with each of these three scenarios.

The fourth scenario, one that most investors don't think of, is that the markets may not open at all. This could be due to weather, power outages, natural disasters etc.

Investors, particularly short-term traders, should have a strategy in place in the event that the markets don't open. This could be the use of ECN's, foreign or regional exchanges, or perhaps the prior implementation of hedging strategies such as options.

Conclusion

I hope you have found this information to be valuable. Although there is never a guarantee against loss, a good knowledge of trading and order types helps make for a more successful stock market investor. Good luck in your trading.

Bill Thompson

Appendix – Historical Currencies of the United States

Here are some examples as to how the paper money of the United States has changed over the years.

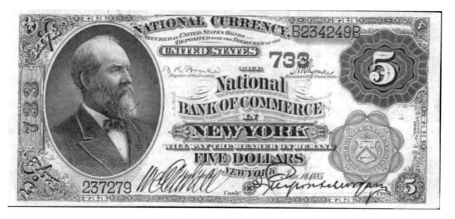

Made in the USA
Monee, IL
15 January 2022

88954310R00052